INDISPENSABLE LEADER CERTIFICATION PROGRAM

PARTICIPANT GUIDE

PRESENTED BY

INDISPENSABLE LEADER CERTIFICATION PROGRAM: PARTICIPANT GUIDE

Copyright © 2018 by StephenK Leadership

All rights reserved. No part of this workbook may be reproduced or transmitted in any form or by any means without written permission from the author.

Printed in the United States of America.

10 9 8 7 6 5 4 3 2

DEDICATION

This participant guide is dedicated to you, the leader. The fact you are holding this participant guide in your hands speaks to your desire to become the leader you were created to be. The fact you are holding this participant guide in your hands speaks to the value you place on equipping yourself to be better tomorrow than you are today. The fact you are holding this participant guide in your hands speaks to your willingness to put in the time, effort, energy, and resources needed to achieve every and any goal you have on your heart to achieve.

The participant guide you hold in your hands represents the very best of the StephenK Leadership Team as a company, and more importantly, the very best of me, as a leader. I have facilitated this certification program at more than 180 small and medium-sized businesses throughout the world, and have certified more than 1,000 leaders. With the completion of each certification program, we made this better. With the certification of each leader, we made this program more robust.

The Indispensable Leader Certification Program participant guide you are now holding in your hands is a compilation of my blood, sweat, and tears, as well as more than three years of trial and error. This participant guide represents the very best of StephenK Leadership right now, but you can rest assured that we will not rest on our laurels. We will strive to become better tomorrow than we are today, just like we're expecting you to strive to become better tomorrow than you are today.

Here's to your continued success!

Dr. Stephen Kalaluhi

THIS INDISPENSABLE LEADER CERTIFICATION PROGRAM PARTICPANT GUIDE BELONGS TO:

_____

TABLE OF CONTENTS

DEDICATION 3
INTRODUCTION 7
VISION BASED DECISION MAKING 9
EFFECTIVE COMMUNICATION 31
HIGH PERFORMANCE CULTURE 47
ENHANCING ORGANIZATIONAL TRUST 65
DELEGATING WITH AUTHORITY 83
CREATING POSITIVE CONFLICT 99
INSPIRE AND MOTIVATE YOUR TEAM 115
STRENGTHENING ORGANIZATIONAL TEAMS 129
ORGANIZATIONAL ACCOUNTABILITY 149
COURAGEOUS LEADERSHIP 165
CONCLUSION 179

INTRODUCTION

"Good leadership consists of showing average people how to do the work of superior people."

– *John D. Rockefeller*

The information contained within the following pages is designed to empower and equip you to become an indispensable leader. As you progress through this training program, you will be challenged and you will be stretched – your mind-set will be challenged, your understanding of what it means to be a leader will be stretched, and who you are as a leader will experience exponential growth that only comes from the increase in understanding you will gain in and through this program, as well as from the application of the principles outlined within this text.

Each section of this program is designed to increase your knowledge of not only leadership theory and application, but also increase your personal capacity and ability to be the very best leader you can be. In addition, each section of this program ends with a challenging, yet important call to practical application – just like anything else in life, the more you practice something and do it well, the more successful you will become in that endeavor. It's been said that mastering a skill requires more than 10,000 hours of practice –

taking part in this program is only the first step of many more to come that will help you master the art and science of leadership.

As you progress through this leadership development program, please continuously remind yourself that leadership is not just something you do, it's something you are…it's something that requires action and commitment and dedication to do well. At the end of the day, you will be the leader you set out to be – so make sure you set your sights high!

Here's to your leadership!

Dr. Stephen Kalaluhi

CEO and Founder

The StephenK Leadership Team

SESSION ONE:

VISION BASED DECISION MAKING

THE ⑦ STEP VISION BASED DECISION MAKING PROCESS

> "The worst decision a leader can make is to not make one."
> — Dr. Stephen Kalaluhi

THE DECISION-MAKING PROCESS DEFINED

Decision making is defined as the process of making choices by setting goals, gathering information, and assessing alternative options to achieve the desired outcome.

WHY VISION BASED DECISION-MAKING?

Vision-based decision making takes the routine definition of the decision-making process one step further and focuses everything on the process to determine whether the decision helps achieve the overall vision of the department, or the organization as a whole.

When vision-based decision making is understood and employed within a department or organization, the driving force behind every decision made becomes, "Will this help me and my team achieve the organization's vision?"

STEP #1:
RECOGNIZE A DECISION MUST BE MADE

KEY CONCEPT

The responsibility of a leader is to make decisions. Do not back down from this responsibility; do not pass it off to someone else; do not hope it will blow over and go away. Make a decision and stick with it.

IMPLEMENTATION

Stay cognizant and aware of what's going on in your organization. The more you know about what is negatively affecting your teams' ability to succeed, the sooner you'll be able to make the decisions that must be made.

PITFALLS

Leading from behind a desk prevents you from fully being connected to what's truly going on in your organization. It is critical that you see for yourself what is affecting the success and growth of your team.

GROWTH CHALLENGE QUESTIONS

1) WHY IS RECOGNIZING A DECISION MUST BE MADE IMPORTANT?

2) WHAT CAN YOU DO TO IMPROVE YOUR ABILITY TO RECOGNIZE WHEN DECISIONS MUST BE MADE?

3) WHAT CAN YOU DO TO AVOID THE PITFALLS ASSOCIATED WITH THIS STEP?

ADDITIONAL NOTES

STEP #2:
IDENTIFY ALL FEASIBLE OPTIONS

KEY CONCEPT

Brainstorm as many feasible ideas and options as possible to create a robust list of solutions. In this step, the more ideas and options listed, the better. Bring in your team to help generate ideas.

IMPLEMENTATION

The key to this step being successful is giving your people enough time to fully consider options. Send your team an email outlining the challenge, then give them a day or two to come up with ideas.

PITFALLS

Ensure your team stays focused on the process being decided upon. This will help reduce the emotional connection people have when it comes to accepting or rejecting ideas and options.

GROWTH CHALLENGE QUESTIONS

1) WHAT IS MORE IMPORTANT IN THIS STEP: QUANTITY OR QUALITY? WHY?

2) WHAT CAN YOU DO TO REMOVE THE EMOTIONAL CONNECTION PEOPLE HAVE WHEN IT COMES TO THEIR IDEAS BEING CHOSEN OR REJECTED?

3) HOW IS GENERATING IDEAS AND OPTIONS LIKE WORKING OUT A MUSCLE?

ADDITIONAL NOTES

STEP #3:
ANALYZE ALL POSSIBLE OUTCOMES

KEY CONCEPT

Narrow down the list created from the last step. Analyze the possible outcomes that each idea or option might produce. Create a list of pros and cons as it relates to the possible results from each idea generated.

IMPLEMENTATION

Empower your team to complete this step. Challenge each team member to analyze their own idea and present to you and the team what might or could happen if their idea is implemented.

PITFALLS

Keep this step within reason. It's way too easy to head off on a tangent with this step. Ensure your team stays focused on the reason they are there, rather than allowing for what could happen to be taken to the extreme.

GROWTH CHALLENGE QUESTIONS

1) HOW MUCH TIME SHOULD YOU ALLOCATE TO THIS STEP?

2) WHAT DOES EMPOWERING YOUR TEAM TO ANALYZE THEIR OWN IDEAS DO FOR THEIR DECISION-MAKING ABILITY?

3) WHAT PRACTICAL STEPS CAN YOU FOLLOW TO ENSURE THIS STEP DOES NOT GET OUT OF CONTROL?

ADDITIONAL NOTES

STEP #4:
DETERMINE ROI FOR EACH VIABLE OPTION

KEY CONCEPT

Determine the return you anticipate from each option listed in the previous step. Identify which option helps you achieve your organizational vision the fastest.

IMPLEMENTATION

Create a rating scale as it pertains to the anticipated ROI for each option. The higher the rating, the more of a return you expect. This process is all about achieving your vision, and the decision must support that.

PITFALLS

The ROI is only valuable to your decision-making process if you are fully aware of your organizational vision. The ROI here must speak in terms of achieving vision the fastest with the least amount of investment.

GROWTH CHALLENGE QUESTIONS

1) WHAT IS YOUR ORGANIZATION'S VISION?

2) HOW DOES KNOWING YOUR ORGANIZATIONAL VISION COME INTO PLAY AS IT RELATES TO DETERMINING ROI FOR EACH OPTION?

3) WHY IS LINKING ROI TO ORGANIZATIONAL VISION SO IMPORTANT TO THE OVERALL GROWTH OF YOUR COMPANY?

ADDITIONAL NOTES

STEP #5:
IMPLEMENT THE AGREED UPON DECISION

KEY CONCEPT

Once you determine which option provides the greatest return on your investment, the next step is to take action. It is in the execution of the decision that leaders separate themselves from those who choose not to act.

IMPLEMENTATION

Decisions without action are worthless. For the work you and your team completed to be of value, you must take action. Hold yourself and your team accountable to executing against the agreed upon plan of action.

PITFALLS

Paralysis by analysis is a very real thing. It has the power to freeze the best leaders in place. Do not allow fear to prevent you from moving forward and from taking the action that you need to take.

GROWTH CHALLENGE QUESTIONS

1) WHY DO YOU THINK LEADERS ARE FEARFUL OF TAKING ACTION ON THEIR DECISIONS?

2) WHAT PRACTICAL STEPS CAN YOU TAKE TO BUILD ACCOUNTABILITY INTO YOUR DECISION-MAKING PROCESS?

3) HOW CAN YOU OVERCOME ANY FEAR ASSOCIATED WITH EXECUTING AGAINST AN AGREED UPON DECISION?

ADDITIONAL NOTES

POINT OF REFLECTION

CONSIDER THIS…

Steps #6 and #7 are what separates good leaders from great leaders. Too many leaders fail to implement these two steps and, as a result, never achieve the success and growth they know they are capable of.

WHAT GETS MEASURED GETS IMPROVED

If you can't measure it, there is no way to make it better. If you can't measure it, there is no way to ensure it can't be done better. If you can't measure it, there is no way to determine how effective your decision truly was.

REASSESS, AS NEEDED

It is very seldom that you will ever make a decision with 100% of the details and information you need to make a great decision. It is important to reassess your decision as more and more information becomes available.

STEP #6:
MEASURE DECISION FOR EFFECTIVENESS

KEY CONCEPT

For you to know how effective your decision-making skills are, you must understand and identify the results and what they mean to the overall growth of your organization.

IMPLEMENTATION

Ask yourself and your team whether the results you are seeing are aligned with the results you expected to see. Evaluate the results to ensure you are seeing and achieving what you expected to see and achieve.

PITFALLS

Create reasonable expectations based on the timeframe from which you are measuring. Your week-long results may not be as impressive as your month-long results. Ensure you match your expectations accordingly.

GROWTH CHALLENGE QUESTIONS

1) WHICH STEP OF THIS PROCESS PROVIDES YOU WITH THE MEASURABLE RESULTS YOU ARE EXPECTING?

2) WHAT CAN YOU DO TO ENSURE YOU ARE MEASURING IN A TIMEFRAME THAT WILL PROVIDE THE MOST VALUABLE INFO?

3) AT WHAT POINT IN THIS PROCESS SHOULD A TIMELINE FOR MEASURING BE ESTABLISHED?

ADDITIONAL NOTES

STEP #7:
REASSESS FOR EFFECTIVENESS, AS NEEDED

KEY CONCEPT

You make the best decisions you possibly can with the information you have available. It is important to remain flexible enough, however, to make the necessary in-course corrections when new information comes to light.

IMPLEMENTATION

It is critical to schedule regular follow-up sessions to review the effectiveness of any decision made. The more the decision affects your organization, the more often you should conduct follow-ups.

PITFALLS

This step must be conducted intentionally and purposefully. It is too easy to ignore this step, but this is the one step that can, and will, transform the effectiveness of your decision-making process.

GROWTH CHALLENGE QUESTIONS

1) WHY DO YOU THINK SO FEW LEADERS PERFORM THIS STEP?

2) IN WHAT WAYS CAN THIS STEP IMPROVE YOUR DECISION-MAKING ABILITY?

3) WHAT CAN YOU DO TO AVOID THE PITFALLS ASSOCIATED WITH THIS STEP?

ADDITIONAL NOTES

SUMMARY:
VISION BASED DECISION MAKING PROCESS

KEY CONCEPT
The 7-Step Vision Based Decision Making Process is powerful because it is rooted in you answering the question, "Will this decision help me and my organization achieve our vision and goals?"

IMPLEMENTATION
This process must be purposeful and intentional. The value of following this process is only found in executing against the 7 steps outlined in this session. Hold yourself and your team accountable to doing this process.

PITFALLS
The responsibility of a leader is to make decisions. Do not back down from this responsibility; do not pass it off to someone else; do not hope it will blow over and go away. Make a decision and stick with it.

ADDITIONAL NOTES

SESSION TWO:

EFFECTIVE COMMUNICATION

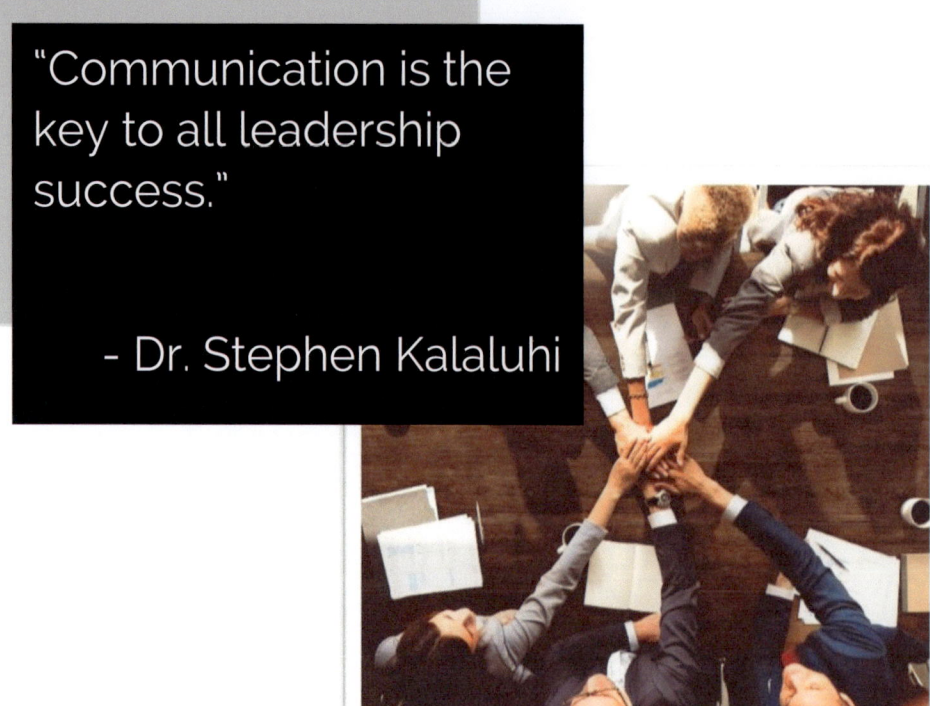

> "Communication is the key to all leadership success."
>
> - Dr. Stephen Kalaluhi

COMMUNICATE BETTER

Your ability to communicate forms the foundation of great leadership. Great leaders can effectively communicate their heart, their vision, and the action steps their team must accomplish to be successful.

EFFECTIVE COMMUNICATION

Great leaders recognize that communication is a learned skill. Great communication deals with more than what is said, it focuses on the emotions behind what is said, as well as the intent with which it is said.

Effective communication is built on nonverbal communication, engaged listening, communicating assertively, and understanding how emotions affect those you are communication with.

③ BARRIERS TO EFFECTIVE COMMUNICATION

3 BARRIERS TO EFFECTIVE COMMUNICATION

UNCONTROLLED EMOTIONS

Uncontrolled stress and unchecked emotions lead to confusing nonverbal signals, as well as unhealthy knee-jerk reactions to what others try to communicate to you.

INCONSISTENT BODY LANGUAGE

Inconsistent body language contradicts what you say, as opposed to reinforcing it. Inconsistent body language creates an environment where others likely perceive the communication to be dishonest.

LACK OF FOCUS

Multitasking is a barrier to successful communication as it leads to thinking about what to say next, as opposed to being fully engaged. This results in you checking emails, text messages, and daydreaming

HOW DO MY EMOTIONS AFFECT MY ABILITY TO COMMUNICATE WELL?

DOES MY BODY LANGUAGE ALIGN WITH WHAT I AM SAYING?

HOW IS MULTITASKING PREVENTING ME FROM SUCCESSFULLY COMMUNICATING?

POINT OF REFLECTION

CONSIDER THIS…

If left unchecked, these three barriers can negate any efforts you make to become a successful and effective leader. Remember, your words are the last thing people "hear" when you communicate.

SO, HOW DO I COMMUNICATE SUCCESSFULLY, THEN?

3 KEYS TO POWERFUL COMMUNICATION

KEY #1: BE AN ENGAGED COMMUNICATOR

① FOCUS FULLY ON WHO IS SPEAKING

This allows you to recognize the tone of voice used, nonverbal cues demonstrated, and body language exhibited. Focusing on who is speaking prevents distractions from preventing you from understanding what is being said.

② AVOID INTERRUPTIONS

Communicating requires more of you than just waiting for your turn to talk. Being engaged is about concentrating on not only what is being said, but also how it is being said.

③ PROVIDE TIMELY FEEDBACK

Powerful communicators ask clarifying questions to ensure the true meaning of the conversation is understood and grasped. This is a critical component of communication as it prevents you from being disconnected from what is being shared.

HOW DOES FULLY FOCUSING ON WHO IS SPEAKING HELP ME STAY ENGAGED?

WHAT CAN I DO TO ENSURE I DO NOT INTERRUPT THE PERSON WHO IS SHARING?

WHAT DOES PROVIDING TIMELY FEEDBACK DURING A CONVERSATION MEAN?

KEY #2: BE AWARE OF NONVERBALS

① ADJUST NONVERBALS TO THE CONTEXT

Considering the emotional state of those you're communicating with allows you to adjust your tone of voice to more appropriately match the situation you're communicating in.

② USE BODY LANGUAGE POSITIVELY

Positive body language conveys confidence, even when you aren't confident. Examples of positive body language include maintaining eye contact, standing with your shoulders back, delivering a firm handshake, and smiling.

③ BE AWARE OF INDIVIDUAL DIFFERENCES

Differences in age, gender, culture, religion, and emotional state determine the effectiveness of nonverbal communication. Stay aware of individual differences even when communicating to large groups.

WHAT IS AN EXAMPLE OF A MISALIGNED NONVERBAL TO ITS CONTEXT?

HOW CAN POSITIVE BODY LANGUAGE HELP ME BECOME MORE CONFIDENT?

WHY ARE INDIVIDUAL DIFFERENCES IN A GROUP SETTING IMPORTANT?

KEY #3: BE ASSERTIVE

① VALUE YOURSELF AND YOUR OPINIONS

Believe that what you have to say will add value to those you are saying it to. Remember that your opinions and your thoughts are as valuable as anyone else's.

② EXPRESS NEGATIVES POSITIVELY

Communicating negative news or negative results can be done in such a way that creates a positive response from those hearing it. Focusing on the positive when you communicate allows you to effectively turn the tides on an otherwise difficult situation or circumstance.

③ LEARN TO SAY, "NO."

Knowing your limits allows you to communicate alternatives to those who place demands on your time and capacity. Communicating when you are taking on too much requires you to assert yourself as a communicator.

HOW DO YOU ENSURE YOUR VOICE IS HEARD ABOVE ALL THE NOISE?

HOW CAN YOU COMMUNICATE THE GOOD IN THE BAD NEWS?

HOW DOES SAYING "NO" FORCE YOU TO COME UP WITH ALTERNATIVE IDEAS?

SUMMARY: EFFECTIVE COMMUNICATION

KEY CONCEPT

Communicating effectively has less to do with the words you choose, as it does with how you say those words. Your body language, your nonverbals, and how well you engage speaks louder than anything you might say.

IMPLEMENTATION

Practice. Instead of trying to implement everything at once, focus on identifying a single area you believe you could do better in. Be cognizant and aware of that one thing until it becomes a part of who you are.

PITFALLS

The barriers that prevent you from effectively communicating are present, but often times not seen. To become powerful communicators, we must be open to feedback from our peers and our leaders regarding what we can do to improve how we communicate.

ADDITIONAL NOTES

SESSION THREE:

CREATING A HIGH PERFORMANCE CULTURE

5 KEYS TO CREATING A HIGH-PERFORMANCE CULTURE

> "High performance culture is built on the backs of high performance leaders."
> - Dr. Stephen Kalaluhi

WHAT IS THE SECRET TO CREATING A HIGH-PERFORMANCE CULTURE?

Every high-performance culture has, at its core, the need to be led by a team of high performance leaders. Mary Kay Ash, founder of Mary Kay Cosmetics, Inc., once said, "The speed of the leader is the speed of the gang." As it relates to creating a high-performance culture, she is absolutely correct. As a leader, you are, and will always be, the limiting factor in how well your team performs, how effectively they communicate, and how adept they are at addressing challenges as they arise. The secret to creating a high-performance culture is you becoming a high-performance leader!

KEY #1:
BE A PROBLEM SOLVER

✓ KEY CONCEPT

It doesn't matter how much influence you exert over an individual, if you're not able to solve the problems that are preventing them from completing their assigned tasks.

➕ IMPLEMENTATION

Being a problems solver is as simple as asking the question, "Is there anything today that could prevent you from meeting or exceeding the expectations I have of you?" Listen to the responses and solve accordingly.

✖ PITFALLS

Being a problem solver takes time, effort, energy, and resources – four things leaders have very little extra of. You must learn to allocate enough of each in order to solve problems as they arise.

GROWTH CHALLENGE QUESTIONS

1) WHY IS SOLVING PROBLEMS CRITICAL TO YOU BEING AN EFFECTIVE LEADER?

2) WHAT IS MORE IMPORTANT, ASKING ABOUT PROBLEMS OR ACTING ON THE PROBLEMS THAT ARE SHARED?

3) HOW CAN YOU ENSURE YOU HAVE THE TIME NEEDED TO EFFECTIVELY SOLVE PROBLEMS AS THEY ARISE?

ADDITIONAL NOTES

KEY #2:
RALLY THE TROOPS

KEY CONCEPT

Engaged employees know the organization's vision, as well as how they affect the successful achievement of that vision in their role. Mobilizing your team then, is the result of sharing your organization's overall vision.

IMPLEMENTATION

Memorize your organization's vision statement. Challenge those on your team to memorize your organization's vision statement. Identify how each team member is crucial to the achievement of the overall vision.

PITFALLS

A compelling vision statement not only engages and mobilizes your people, it motivates and inspires them to excel, as well. Revise your vision statement so that it is inspiring enough to get you out of bed each day.

GROWTH CHALLENGE QUESTIONS

1) HOW DOES SHARING THE ORG'S VISION HELP GET PEOPLE FROM WHERE THEY ARE NOW, TO WHERE YOU NEED THEM TO BE?

2) STATE YOUR ORGANIZATION'S VISION STATEMENT IN THE SPACE BELOW.

3) IS YOUR VISION STATEMENT COMPELLING ENOUGH TO GET YOU OUT OF BED? IF NOT, REVISE IT HERE.

ADDITIONAL NOTES

KEY #3: COLLABORATE OR DIE

KEY CONCEPT

Collaboration focuses on tapping into the strengths of every member of your team. You might be good at what you do, but you'll never be as good as when you ask others for their input and opinions.

IMPLEMENTATION

Ask your team members how they would improve their systems and processes if they were given the opportunity to do so. Create a space for them to share their ideas on how to improve their areas of responsibility.

PITFALLS

At the end of the day, you are responsible for the quality of the choices and ideas that your team generates. Never abdicate the responsibility of choosing what to implement to your team. Their opinions, your decision.

GROWTH CHALLENGE QUESTIONS

1) IDENTIFY LEADERS ON YOUR TEAM WHOM YOU CAN RELY ON TO PROVIDE INSIGHTS REGARDING AREAS OF IMPROVEMENT.

2) TASK THE LEADERS LISTED ABOVE TO GENERATE IDEAS REGARDING WHAT THEY WOULD DO TO IMPROVE THEIR AREAS.

3) UTILIZE THE VISION BASED DECISION MAKING PROCESS TO IMPLEMENT THE IDEA WITH THE GREATEST ROI.

ADDITIONAL NOTES

KEY #4:
STRATEGY MADE SIMPLE

KEY CONCEPT

Your organizational strategy must support the achievement of your organizational vision. Professional, personal, and financial growth goals must all point to how your organization will achieve its overall vision.

IMPLEMENTATION

What is your professional, personal, and financial growth goal for the rest of this year? What do you have to do as an organization to achieve it? This answer becomes your organization's strategic plan.

PITFALLS

Strategy should not be overly complicated or complex. The simpler your strategy for success is, the more people in your organization can understand it and own it.

GROWTH CHALLENGE QUESTIONS

1) WHAT ARE YOUR PROFESSIONAL, PERSONAL, AND FINANCIAL GROWTH GOALS FOR THE REMAINDER OF THIS YEAR?

2) WHAT DO YOU NEED TO DO TO ACHIEVE EACH OF THESE THREE GOALS BY THE END OF THIS YEAR?

3) COMMUNICATE THIS STRATEGIC PLAN TO YOUR TEAM.

ADDITIONAL NOTES

KEY #5:
KEEP THEM MOVING

KEY CONCEPT

Protecting the momentum of the growth you and your organization are experiencing is critical to continued success. Creating a high-performance culture is predicated on you protecting what you've already built.

IMPLEMENTATION

Address any negative talk or attitudes immediately. Keep your people focused on their growth and why their growth is critical to achieving the organization's overarching vision.

PITFALLS

It only takes one negative person to derail your efforts to create a high-performance culture. You must not only protect the momentum, but you must also shield your team from negative thoughts and comments of others.

GROWTH CHALLENGE QUESTIONS

1) WHY IS IT IMPORTANT THAT YOU ADDRESS NEGATIVITY IMMEDIATELY IN A HIGH-PERFORMANCE CULTURE?

2) WHAT STEPS CAN YOU TAKE TO ENSURE NEGATIVITY DOES NOT AFFECT THOSE WITHIN YOUR ORGANIZATION?

3) WHAT ACTIONS SHOULD YOU TAKE WHEN DEALING WITH INDIVIDUALS WHO CHOOSE TO SPREAD NEGATIVITY?

ADDITIONAL NOTES

POINTS OF REFLECTION

CONSIDER THIS...

A high-performance culture is the direct result of high-performance leaders. If you want to establish a high-performance culture in your organization, you must become a high-performance leader. What are you going to do today to become a high-performance leader? What are you going to do to sustain the level of leadership needed to create a high-performance culture within your organization?

GROWTH MUST HAPPEN DAILY

If there's any hope of your organization being better tomorrow than it is today, you must be better tomorrow. Creating a mindset of continuous growth and development is the key to building an organization founded upon learning. You cannot rest on your laurels or your past successes if you desire to achieve continued success.

ACCOUNTABILITY IS KING

Your organization won't do what you expect, they will only do what you inspect. It is critically important to the growth of your organization that you trust your team to do what they need to do, but verify that it is being done. Metrics and weekly reports must speak to what your organization did to grow.

SUMMARY: CREATING A HIGH-PERFORMANCE CULTURE

KEY CONCEPT

What you do as a leader will determine how long your organization takes to shift its mindset to one of continuous growth and continuous development. You determine the speed, as well as how far it all will go.

IMPLEMENTATION

You must hold your organization, and yourself, accountable for growth. Don't set expectations if you have no plan in place to inspect the results. Measured growth is what matters most.

PITFALLS

Creating a high-performance culture takes time, it takes commitment, and it takes people willing to do whatever it takes to grow. Your vision becomes an important factor in the success of this component.

ADDITIONAL NOTES

SESSION FOUR:

ENHANCING ORGANIZATIONAL TRUST

7 KEYS TO ENHANCING ORGANIZATIONAL TRUST

> "You must trust your people, and your people must trust you."
>
> - Dr. Stephen Kalaluhi

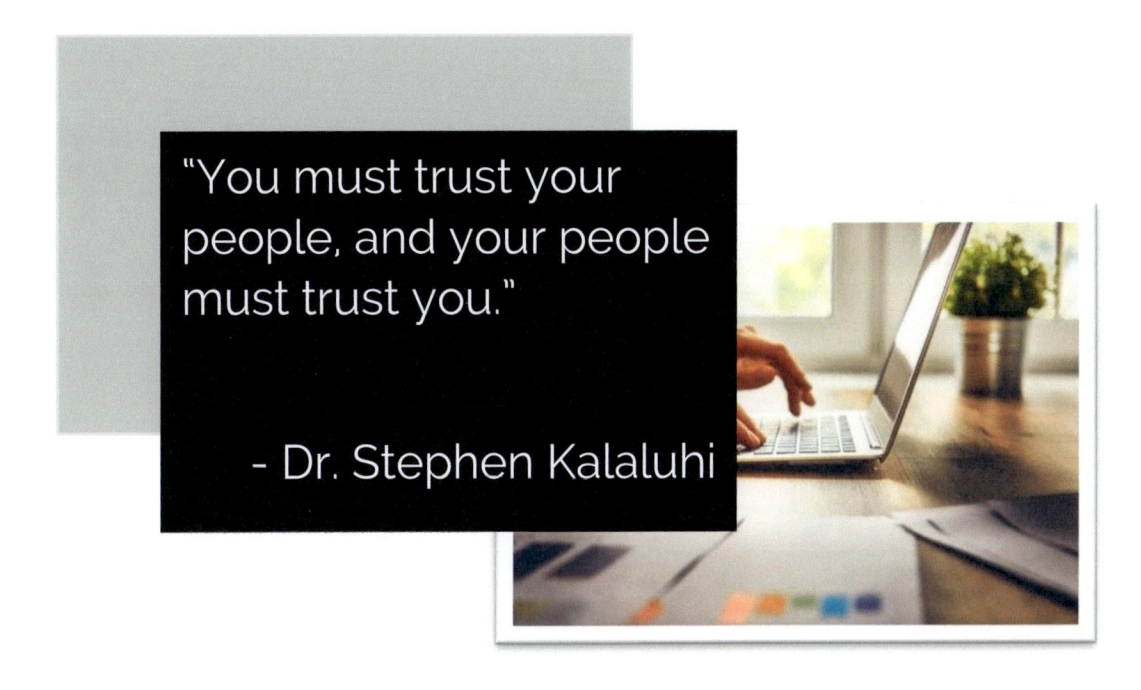

ENHANCING ORGANIZATIONAL TRUST

Trust allows you to bridge the gap between where your people are now and where you need them to be to succeed as an organization. Much has been written about on the positive effects of developing and maintaining high levels of trust, and this section focuses on those practical aspects that you must master to develop and protect the trust that your people have in you.

Trust is the natural byproduct of developing relationships with your people, and developing relationships with your people is the natural byproduct of knowing who you are leading. Where many leaders fail is in the knowing. Great leaders are willing to invest the time and effort needed to go deeper, and to effectively lead those within their organization.

KEY #1:

KEY:

Trusted leaders understand their people on both a personal and professional level.

WHY THIS IS IMPORTANT:

The biggest challenge leaders face when building relationships with their people is creating that fine line between business life and personal life. Because the line is so thin, many leaders shy away from even broaching the personal side of the people they lead. Great leaders, however, successfully merge the two by setting ground rules and boundaries that let their people know when it's appropriate to discuss their personal lives and when it's time to focus on work.

HOW WELL DO I KNOW THE PEOPLE ON MY TEAM?

WHAT BOUNDARIES CAN I CREATE TO FACILITATE KNOWING THEM BETTER?

HOW WELL DO MY PEOPLE KNOW ME?

KEY #2:

KEY:

Trusted leaders assess their relationships with each team member.

WHY THIS IS IMPORTANT:

Being real with yourself and the strength of the relationships you have with your people is a critical component of becoming a great leader. If you aren't open to assessing your current relationships, then you won't be open to what it's going to take to improve those relationships. Great leaders effectively reflect on the strength of each relationship so that they can understand what needs to be worked on to improve trust within the organization.

WHY DO YOU THINK SOME RELATIONSHIPS ARE STRONGER THAN OTHERS?

WHAT CAN YOU DO TO STRENGTHEN THOSE WEAKER RELATIONSHIPS?

WHY IS THIS KEY IMPORTANT TO ENHANCING TRUST?

KEY #3:

KEY:

Trusted leaders take the necessary steps to strengthen their relationships.

WHY THIS IS IMPORTANT:

Assessing the strength of each of your relationships is key, but that exercise pales in comparison to taking action to improve each relationship. Executing a plan allows great leaders to build on their relationships, as well as keep their fingers on the pulse of their people.

CREATE A PLAN DESIGNED TO ENHANCE EACH OF YOUR RELATIONSHIPS.

HOW WILL YOU IMPLEMENT THE PLAN?

HOW WILL THIS PLAN BENEFIT YOUR TEAM?

KEY #4:

KEY:

Trusted leaders identify their powerbase within the organization.

WHY THIS IS IMPORTANT:

Your powerbase is comprised of several people: Strong Supporters, Neutral Parties, Antagonists, Nemeses, and Strangers. Each role has a place in the success of your organization, but it is only through the building of relationships are you able to accurately identify who falls into which category.

IDENTIFY YOUR STRONG SUPPORTERS.

IDENTIFY YOUR ANTAGONISTS.

IN WHAT CONTEXTS WOULD ONE BE PREFERRED OVER THE OTHER?

KEY #5:

KEY:

Trusted leaders customize their leadership approach to the individual.

WHY THIS IS IMPORTANT:

Great leaders understand the importance of leading the person, instead of leading the group. One person may need you to be direct, while another may need you to be more hands-off. Your success as a leader is determined by how well you match your leadership style to the person you're leading. This kind of knowledge and insight only comes from building relationships with your people.

HOW MANY DIRECT REPORTS DO YOU HAVE IN YOUR ORGANIZATION?

WHAT LEADERSHIP STYLE DOES EACH PERSON ON YOUR TEAM PREFER?

ESTABLISH A TIMELINE TO DETERMINE WHICH FOR THOSE YOU DO NOT KNOW.

KEY #6:

KEY:

Trusted leaders make space for their people to give regular feedback.

WHY THIS IS IMPORTANT:

Relationships in the workplace build trust because people are more willing to give feedback when they trust you won't overreact or punish them for their opinions. Great leaders make space for their people to give feedback, meaning it is scheduled and there is a system in place to receive and respond to their insight and feedback.

WHAT IS STOPPING YOU FROM ALLOWING FEEDBACK FROM YOUR TEAM?

WHAT SYSTEMS CAN YOU IMPLEMENT TO SUPPORT CONTINUOUS FEEDBACK?

WHAT HAPPENS IF YOU DISAGREE WITH TEAM FEEDBACK?

KEY #7:

KEY:

Trusted leaders develop their people for future growth.

WHY THIS IS IMPORTANT:

Building relationships allows you to better understand your people's goals, desires, and dreams not only within the organization, but for their lives as a whole. Knowing what each employee wants out of their career gives you the ability to assign people to projects based on what they enjoy doing and where they want to progress. Great leaders match their people to the task based on what they like doing and what they are good at doing.

IDENTIFY THE PROFESSIONAL ASPIRATIONS OF EACH TEAM MEMBER.

IDENTIFY THE PERSONAL ASPIRATIONS OF EACH TEAM MEMBER.

WHAT CAN YOU DO TO HELP EACH MEMBER ACHIEVE THEIR ASPIRATIONS?

SUMMARY: ENHANCING ORGANIZATIONAL TRUST

KEY CONCEPT

Trust is developed as the direct result of strengthened relationships. The stronger your relationships, the more trust you will build. Enhancing trust within your organization, then, is a matter of enhancing relationships.

IMPLEMENTATION

Enhancing trust within your organization requires intentional and purposeful action on your part. You must get to know your team so that you can effectively lead them.

PITFALLS

This section is arguably the most challenging in terms of implementation It takes time and an investment of your resources to do well. However, the results are well worth your investment.

SESSION FIVE:

DELEGATING WITH AUTHORITY

6 STRATEGIES TO DELEGATE WITH AUTHORITY

> "The ability to delegate is directly correlated to your ability to succeed. Success is linked to delegation."
>
> - Dr. Stephen Kalaluhi

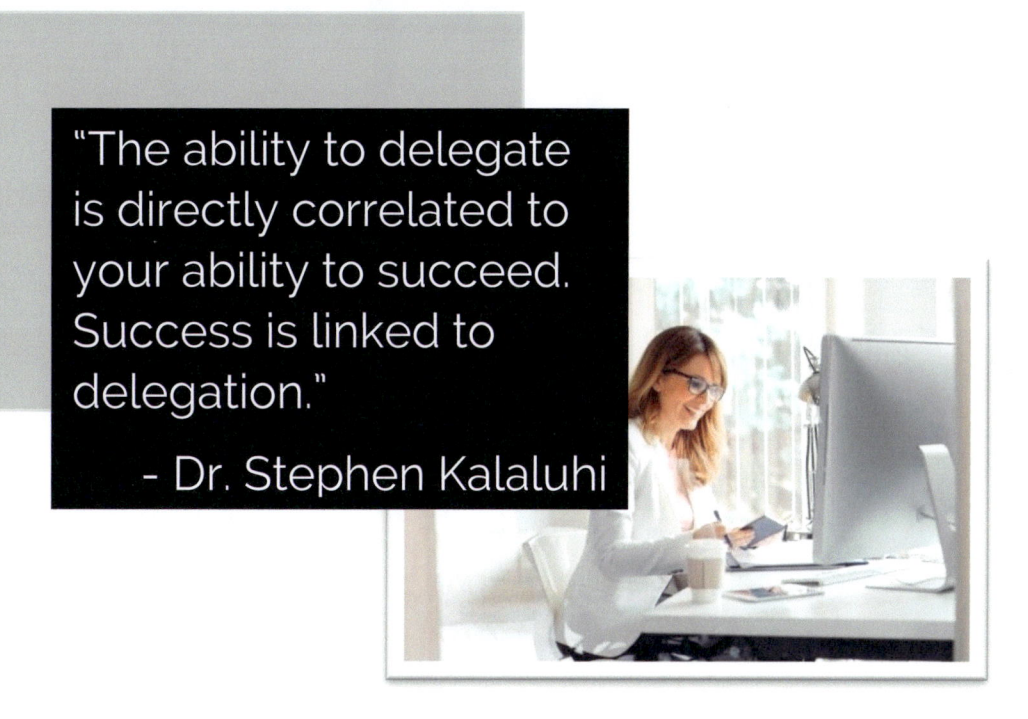

DELEGATING WITH AUTHORITY

Learning to delegate is a key leadership skill set that must be mastered in order to unlock organizational potential. The inability to delegate contributes to limitations in the growth and increase of not only the leaders of your company, but in your entire organization as a whole.

As a leadership skill set, the ability to successfully delegate is mastered only after creating an environment of trust. The more you trust your team, the easier it becomes to delegate. The six strategies discussed in the following section provide you with practical steps you can implement to increase your ability to delegate with authority.

STRATEGY # ① :

Let It Go

- Learning to delegate well starts with being able to let it go.
- Letting go often starts with believing that others can accomplish what needs to be done in the timeframe you need it done by.
- Trusting your team to do what it needs to do is crucial to delegating well.
- Increasing your levels of trust is the beginning of successfully delegating.

IMPLEMENTING STRATEGY #①:

How to Let It Go

- To build confidence levels from within your team, select a low risk task to delegate.
- Be okay with failure.
- Use failure as a teachable moment.
- Know that your team is not going to complete the task the same way you would complete it – be okay with that.
- Recognize that your team is learning how to appease you while you are simultaneously learning how to delegate well.

STRATEGY # ② :

Prioritize the Delegated Tasks

- Delegating with authority means equipping and directing those on your team to succeed.
- To accomplish this, you must communicate priorities and let your team know what must be done first.
- They need you to communicate which task is most important.

IMPLEMENTING STRATEGY #2:

How to Prioritize the Delegated Tasks

- You determine what needs to be done and by when.
- Do not make your team read your mind as it relates to when each task needs to be completed.
- Set your team up to succeed when you delegate with authority.

STRATEGY # ③:

Know Your Team

- When you understand which team members possess which strengths, it becomes easier to delegate.
- When you know the strengths of your team, you can assign tasks based on who does each task the best.

IMPLEMENTING STRATEGY # ③:

Getting to Know Your Team

- Ask.
- Aspirations, goals, dreams…knowing this about your team will give you insight pertaining to who wants to do what, and when.
- Talents, skills, and abilities…create a chart for quick reference.

STRATEGY # ④:

Give Clear Directions

- The clearer your directions, the more capable your team will become.
- When it comes to developing the skill sets needed to master delegation, the clearer you are as a leader, the more effective your team becomes at achieving the goal.
- Remember that ambiguity destroys your ability to delegate with authority.

IMPLEMENTING STRATEGY # ④:

How to Give Clear Directions

- When does it need to be completed by?
- To whom can your team turn to if they run into challenges?
- What progress checks do you want implemented?
- How often do you want your team to check in with you?
- How do you want to your team to communicate timeline challenges?
- At what point will you step in to lend a helping hand?

STRATEGY # ⑤:
Train Your Team

- Delegating with authority means providing your team with the training it needs to successfully accomplish the task you are assigning to them.
- You must know who your team is, as well as recognize the strengths and skills they already possess.
- You must also identify which skills they lack, and do whatever you must to strengthen those weaker, but necessary skills.

IMPLEMENTING STRATEGY #5:

Training Your Team

- This is scary to some, but everything you know how to do, your team should know how to do…literally, everything.
- Pay for certifications, licenses, association memberships. Whatever will make your team even more effective than they are right now.
- Specialized skills, hands-on learning, or just being in the know…you must duplicate yourself before you can delegate with authority.

STRATEGY # ⑥:
Trust, but Verify

- Delegating with authority does not remove the need for you to verify your teams' work.
- As a leader, you are required to inspect the work of your team.
- Delegation of tasks does not remove you from being responsible for the quality of the work your team submits.

IMPLEMENTING STRATEGY #6:

Trusting, but Verifying

- Build into your project timeline a grace period that allows for inspection.
- Build into your project timeline a grace period that allows for corrections to be made.
- Use identified revisions as teachable moments…help your team see what you see so they can avoid the same things in future projects.

SESSION SIX:

CREATING POSITIVE CONFLICT

6

STEPS TO CREATE POSITIVE CONFLICT

> "Positive conflict is the precursor to organizational growth."
>
> - Dr. Stephen Kalaluhi

IS POSITIVE CONFLICT A REAL THING?

Many organizations turn a blind eye to conflict within their teams because they simply are not equipped or trained to effectively resolve the conflict. This training session addresses how to effectively neutralize conflict within your organization, turning it into something your company welcomes instead of runs from.

Research has found that 85% of those who participated in a recent research study stated they dealt with workplace conflict on a regular or frequent basis. That same study found that employees spent almost three hours each week dealing with the negative effects of conflict within the workplace.

While conflict has a negative connotation associated with it when speaking about organizations, this session will show you how to turn those negative effects into positive organizational growth.

STEP # ① :

Open a Dialogue

WHY?

One of the first things to deteriorate when conflict occurs is communication.

and...

HOW?

The first key to resolving conflict and turning its negative effects into positive organizational growth requires you to make space for dialogue to occur. Making space involves creating a safe environment, setting ground rules, and agreeing to the outcome before you attempt to resolve the conflict.

Your Thoughts...

WHY IS COMMUNICATION A CRITICAL FIRST STEP TO THIS PROCESS?

WHAT CAN YOU DO TO CREATE A SAFE ENVIRONMENT FOR DIALOGUE TO OCCUR?

STEP # ②:

Actively Listen

WHY?

Active listening doesn't mean agreeing with what is being said; it means understanding what the other person is saying, feeling, and perceiving.

and...

HOW?

Active listening requires participants to remain present, to not day-dream, to stay focused on what the other person is saying. It's important to recognize that active listening is not a skill that comes naturally to most people. It requires people to ask for clarification, ask probing questions, and to not let go of issues that aren't fully clarified.

Your Thoughts...

HOW CAN I ACTIVELY LISTEN EVEN IF I DON'T AGREE WITH WHAT IS SAID?

WHAT ARE SOME THINGS I CAN DO TO ENSURE IDEAS ARE FULLY CLARIFIED?

STEP # ③:

Process, Not Person

WHY?

Conflict typically stems from a disagreement on process, then escalates because the disagreement is taken personally.

and...

HOW?

When the focus of a conflict within your organization shifts from being about a person to being about what is best for the organization, those involved are more apt to hear what others have to say. When it is not about any one person, all the history and drama is removed and both sides are more able to see what is most beneficial to the organization.

Your Thoughts...

WHAT CAN I DO TO ENSURE ALL INVOLVED FOCUS ON THE PROCESS?

HOW DOES FOCUSING ON THE PROCESS PREVENT PERSONAL ATTACKS?

STEP # ④:

Agree to Disagree

WHY?

Positive conflict does not mean that there is no disagreement.

and...

HOW?

Resolving conflict does not require every person on your team to agree with each other. On the contrary, positive conflict allows for disagreements to occur. The ability to disagree but still move forward is the surest sign of positive conflict within your organization.

Your Thoughts...

EXPLAIN WHY DISAGREEMENTS ARE A GOOD SIGN.

HOW CAN YOU USE DISAGREEMENTS TO MAKE YOUR ORGANIZATION STRONGER?

STEP # ⑤:

Prioritize Resolution

WHY?

Nothing is more important to the overall health and success of your organization than resolving conflict.

and...

HOW?

As a leader, you must do whatever it takes to resolve conflict and turn it into positive organizational growth. Conflict can derail even the best of companies, and it is your responsibility to take the information you gain from opening a dialogue, actively listening, and focusing on the process, and apply it to guiding your team to full and complete resolution.

Your Thoughts...

WHY IS PRIORITIZING THE RESOLUTION A CRITICAL COMPONENT OF THIS PROCESS?

IDENTIFY PRACTICAL ACTIONS YOU CAN TAKE TO ENSURE CONFLICT RESOLUTION IS A PRIORITY IN YOUR ORGANIZATION.

STEP # ⑥ :
Create a Plan

WHY?

Your plan identifies how you will implement and execute positive conflict within your organization. Your strategic plan will drive how the negative effects of conflict will be transformed into positive organizational growth.

and...

HOW?

Now that you have prioritized which areas you and your team will address first, the next step is to create a plan of action. You must ensure that those involved understand what is expected from them, how often they must meet, what the outputs are from those meetings, and how they will report progress to you moving forward.

Your Thoughts...

WHAT IS THE IMPORTANCE OF HAVING A PLAN TO CREATING POSITIVE CONFLICT?

IDENTIFY ADDITIONAL DELIVERABLES AS IT PERTAINS TO IMPLEMENTING THE AGREED UPON PLAN.

SESSION SEVEN:

INSPIRE AND MOTIVATE YOUR TEAM

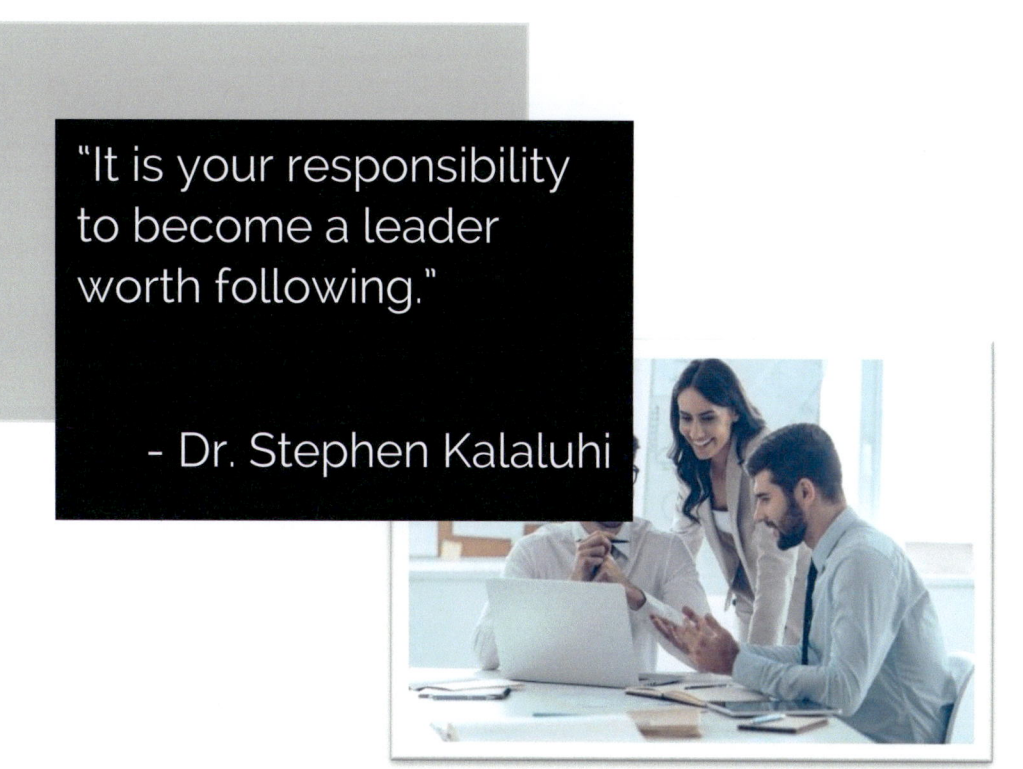

> "It is your responsibility to become a leader worth following."
>
> - Dr. Stephen Kalaluhi

TO MOTIVE // DEFINED

v. To provide an incentive; to move to action; to impel someone to do something.

TO INSPIRE // DEFINED

v. To stimulate to action; to affect or guide; to increase energies, ideals, or reverence.

There is a subtle, but crucial difference between these two words. Often organizational leaders fail to distinguish between the two, which creates frustration and stress related to underperforming individuals and teams. This session will not only shed light on these differences, but it will also share when each is appropriate to use as a leader.

EXTERNALLY DRIVEN

Motivation is the process you follow as a leader to get your team started, to keep them going once they get started, and to keep them focused on achieving a specific and time-bound goal.

INTERNALLY DRIVEN

Inspiration is the process you follow as a leader to help your team imagine something better, to dream about what could be. Imagining something better is the first step to achieving it, and dreaming about what could be is the first step to making it a reality.

Motivation is what you exert on your team as a leader. When you persuade your team to meet a goal, you are motivating them to achieve it. Typically, external motivation is derived from either reward or punishment (e.g. bonuses, loss of job, demotion due to poor performance, etc.).

Inspiration is that drive within your team members to excel, to flourish, and to thrive for no reason other than being better tomorrow than they were today. Internal inspiration results in actions that are owned by the individual. These actions will be achieved with or without your help, and are typically difficult to diminish.

Your Thoughts...

IN YOUR OWN WORDS, DESCRIBE WHAT MOTIVATION IS.

IN YOUR OWN WORDS, DESCRIBE HOW INSPIRATION DIFFERS FROM MOTIVATION.

TO MOTIVATE

or

TO INSPIRE?

DESCRIPTION OF A MOTIVATIONAL LEADER

Motivational leaders are typically exclusively results-driven leaders. These leaders persuade their teams to increase productivity by dangling carrots in front of their noses to increase productivity or improve performance. Motivational leaders are often more concerned with achieving the task than anything else and will employ any tactic necessary to coerce their team to meet or exceed the expectations.

LEADERSHIP BEHAVIORS

- Drives teams for short-term successes using rewards and punishments
- Incentivizes higher productivity and increases in output
- Learns what motivates the individuals on their teams and personalizes rewards / punishments to the individual
- Justifies the means by focusing on the ends

WHEN IS MOTIVATIONAL LEADERSHIP APPROPRIATE?

Motivational leadership, and the behaviors that support it, are most effective when dealing with short-term bursts of needed energy, and when focused on repetitive tasks.

DOWNSIDES OF MOTIVATIONAL LEADERSHIP

It is important for organizational leaders to understand the boundaries associated with motivational leadership. When employed for short-term needs, motivational leadership behaviors are an effective method for getting done what needs to get done. Over a longer period of time, however, motivational leadership behaviors can exhaust employees who can't see the light at the end of the tunnel. Giving 110% is great for a short period of time, but it doesn't take long before your organization starts to fall apart. Utilizing a motivational leadership style and its associated behaviors long-term has the opposite desired effect: Unproductive employees with poor long-term performance.

DESCRIPTION OF AN INSPIRATIONAL LEADER

As opposed to motivational leaders, who focus on accomplishing a task through rewards / punishments, inspriational leaders focus more on the personal growth, professional improvement, and positive outlook of the individuals on their team. Inspirational leaders create high performance teams that are sustainable over the long-term by building challenging environments and cultures that cause individuals to stretch, increase, and get better daily, both personally and professionally. This culture is the precusor to sustainable and reproducible organizational growth.

LEADERSHIP BEHAVIORS

- Design and communicate a clear pathway to achieve long-term growth
- Cultivate a culture of optimism
- Focuses team energy on a worthwhile goal or objective
- Continuously helps team members evolve into stronger and more independent versions of themselves

WHEN IS INSPIRATIONAL LEADERSHIP APPROPRIATE?

Inspirational leadership, and the behaviors that support it, are most effective when shifting an organization's culture, or improving an organization's environment.

DOWNSIDES OF INSPIRATIONAL LEADERSHIP

Of the very few downsides associated with inspirational leadership, the one that causes most leaders to trip is the amount of effort, time, and resources it requires to do well. To inspire each individual on your team requires time, it requires effort on your part to get to know each member, and it means you understand not only their professional goals, but also their personal aspirations. Getting to this point as a leader requires an investment of time and energy; some leaders try to be inspirational without truly understanding what is involved or required, only to fail in the end.

An Open Letter to Leaders...

Dear Leader,

In order to motivate and inspire us, you must have accomplished something motivational and inspiring in your own past. You can't lead us to a place you've never been. In order for our team to view you as a credible leader worth following, you must have accomplished something in your past worthy of generating that motivation and inspiration in me.

You must successfully motivate and inspire us to fully buy-in to the vision of the organization. To do this means you must eat, sleep, breathe, and bleed the vision. It means you never get to turn off being a leader. When we are able to recognize how committed you are to living an inspired life, we will subconsciously pattern our day-to-day lives to match yours.

We are looking for someone worthy of being followed. Your title as our leader will only get you so far. Motivating and inspiring us to reach for more is what will set you apart as a leader worthy of being followed.

Sincerely and with much respect,

Your Team

Your Thoughts...

GIVE AN EXAMPLE OF WHEN ONE STYLE OF LEADERSHIP IS BETTER THAN THE OTHER.

WHAT ARE YOUR THOUGHTS ON THE OPEN LETTER FROM THE PREVIOUS PAGE?

SESSION EIGHT:

STRENGTHENING ORGANIZATIONAL TEAMS

8 KEYS TO STRENGTHENING ORGANIZATIONAL TEAMS

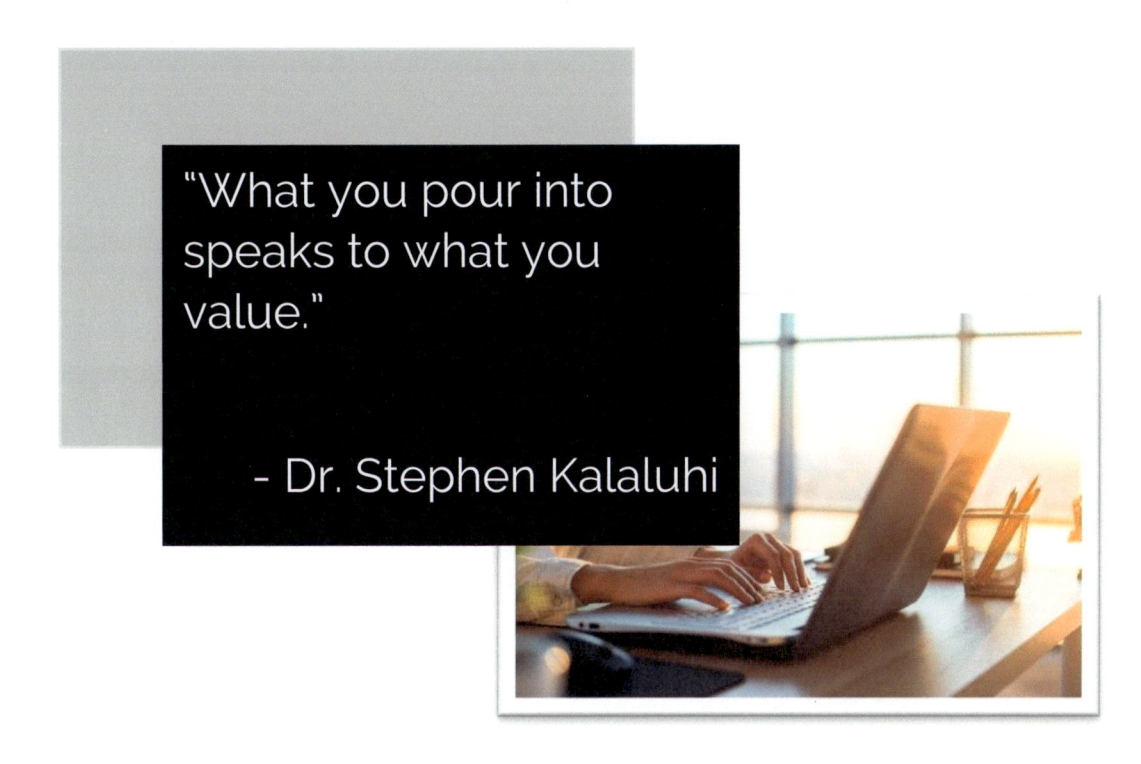

> "What you pour into speaks to what you value."
>
> - Dr. Stephen Kalaluhi

STRENGTHENED RELATIONSHIPS

Strengthening the relationships with those on your team is a critical behavior that you must master if you desire to grow and develop into a leader capable of creating real and lasting change within your organization. This is one area where many leaders talk a great game, but very few leaders follow through on the steps required to build relationships.

This session is designed to jump start your relationship building efforts. It focuses on eight specific areas of leadership that are tantamount to not only building a strong team, but to maintaining it, as well.

KEY #1:

KEY:

It's all about the one-on-one time.

WHY THIS IS IMPORTANT:

You can't strengthen your relationships with your spouse or kids if you're always in the middle of a crowded room. The same principle applies to your team. You must intentionally and purposefully calendar one-on-one time with each team member for the sole purpose of getting to know them better.

Time to Implement

CALENDAR 15 MIN SESSIONS WITH EACH MEMBER OF YOUR TEAM.

IDENTIFY SOMEONE TO HOLD YOU ACCOUNTABLE FOR THESE MEETINGS.

KEY #2:

KEY:

Clear communications.

WHY THIS IS IMPORTANT:

Strengthening the relationships within your team is next to impossible when what you want and what you need is poorly communicated. As a leader, you bring to light those things that are important, and when those things are clearly communicated, everyone on your team is aligned with the goal of moving forward. Aligned team members are strong team members.

Time to Implement

ASK YOUR TEAM WHAT SPECIFIC DETAILS THEY NEED FROM YOU TO SUCCEED IN THEIR ROLES.

CREATE A STRATEGY TO ENSURE YOUR TEAM GETS THE INFO THEY NEED.

KEY #3:

KEY:

It is important to know what is important to the individuals on your team.

WHY THIS IS IMPORTANT:

Is someone on your team learning a new skill? Celebrate them when it is mastered. Is someone on your team going back to school? Celebrate their decision to improve themselves! Knowing what is important to the individuals on your team makes it simpler for you to celebrate those things they consider important. Never forgetting a team member's birthday goes a long way in strengthening the relationships within your team.

Time to Implement

ON AN INDIVIDUAL BASIS, ASK EACH TEAM MEMBER WHAT'S IMPORTANT TO THEM.

CREATE A LIST OF ALL TEAM MEMBER BIRTHDAYS, WORKPLACE ANNIVERSARIES, ETC.

KEY #4:

KEY:

Actively listen to them when they speak.

WHY THIS IS IMPORTANT:

One of the hardest skills to master as a leader and a manager is the ability to actively listen. Active listening is so much deeper than merely hearing what is said. It is about connecting with the person who is speaking, asking clarifying questions when you aren't sure what you heard is what they meant, and summarizing what was shared when the other person is done speaking. To do this well takes time, effort, energy, and focus, but the payoff of strong relationships is absolutely worth it.

Time to Implement

FOR THE NEXT WEEK, PUT ASIDE ANY DISTRACTIONS DURING ALL CONVERSATIONS.

AT THE END OF THE WEEK, JOURNAL HERE REGARDING YOUR EXPERIENCES.

KEY #5:

KEY:

Be the calm, not the storm.

WHY THIS IS IMPORTANT:

Strengthening your relationships is predicated on your ability to keep your team calm, instead of feeding into the chaos. When the craziness of life and work meet head on, you want to be water to the flames instead of being gasoline. You keeping a calm head on your shoulders shows your team they can rely on you to be the voice of reason, allowing them to trust you even more.

Time to Implement

CREATE A STRATEGY TO HELP YOU REMAIN CALM IN THE MIDST OF CHAOS.

SHARE THIS STRATEGY WITH YOUR TEAM AND IDENTIFY SOMEONE TO HOLD YOU ACCOUNTABLE.

KEY #6:

KEY:

Step up when you are in the wrong.

WHY THIS IS IMPORTANT:

The harsh truth of the matter is no one is perfect, to include you. Knowing this truth makes it easier to get things done because you are no longer holding yourself, or your team, to standards you and they can't possibly meet. When you are wrong, and every time you are wrong, own up to the error quickly and do whatever it takes to mend any damage caused by your error.

Time to Implement

OPENLY APOLOGIZE FOR ANY AREAS IN WHICH YOU RECENTLY FAILED.

CREATE A STRATEGY TO ENSURE THE FAILURE DOES NOT OCCUR AGAIN.

KEY #7:

KEY:

Prioritize the relationship, not the work.

WHY THIS IS IMPORTANT:

With deadlines and goals and everything that goes into making your operation run, it is easy to get caught up in the work at the expense of the relationship. Each goal is tied to a person; each deadline is connected to a person; your day-to-day activities are tied to people. Remembering that these things are tied to people helps you strengthen your relationships because, after all, relationships are tied to people, too.

Time to Implement

TAKE YOUR TEAM OUT TO LUNCH BUT DO NOT TALK ABOUT WORK.

OPENLY THANK EACH INDIVIDUAL ON YOUR TEAM FOR THEIR ROLE IN YOUR ORGANIZATION'S SUCCESS.

KEY #8:

KEY:

Walk a mile in their shoes first.

WHY THIS IS IMPORTANT:

The saying goes that you should never mock a person until you've walked a mile in their shoes first. Strengthening relationships is about getting to know your teammates, and getting to know your teammates is about understanding what they're going through and what they are dealing with. As good as people want to believe they are, performance is negatively affected by their personal struggles. Building relationships is about you knowing your people, and providing solutions to whatever might prevent them from achieving their professional goals.

Time to Implement

EACH DAY ASK, "IS THERE ANYTHING IN YOUR PERSONAL LIFE THAT WOULD PREVENT YOU FROM ACHIEVING YOUR PROFESSIONAL GOALS TODAY?"

IF NO, GREAT. IF YES, PROVIDE SOLUTIONS TO THOSE CHALLENGES.

SESSION NINE:

BUILDING ORGANIZATIONAL ACCOUNTABILITY

6 KEYS TO BUILDING ORGANIZATIONAL ACCOUNTABILITY

"You must own your growth; you must own everything you have control over; you must own everything you have no control over."

- Dr. Stephen Kalaluhi

THE ACCOUNTABILITY EPIDEMIC

It's everyone else's fault but the person in charge. No one takes responsibility for failures and shortcomings. People are quick to point fingers and assign blame. This is the accountability epidemic, and it's infecting your organization.

WHY IS ACCOUNTABILITY LACKING TODAY?

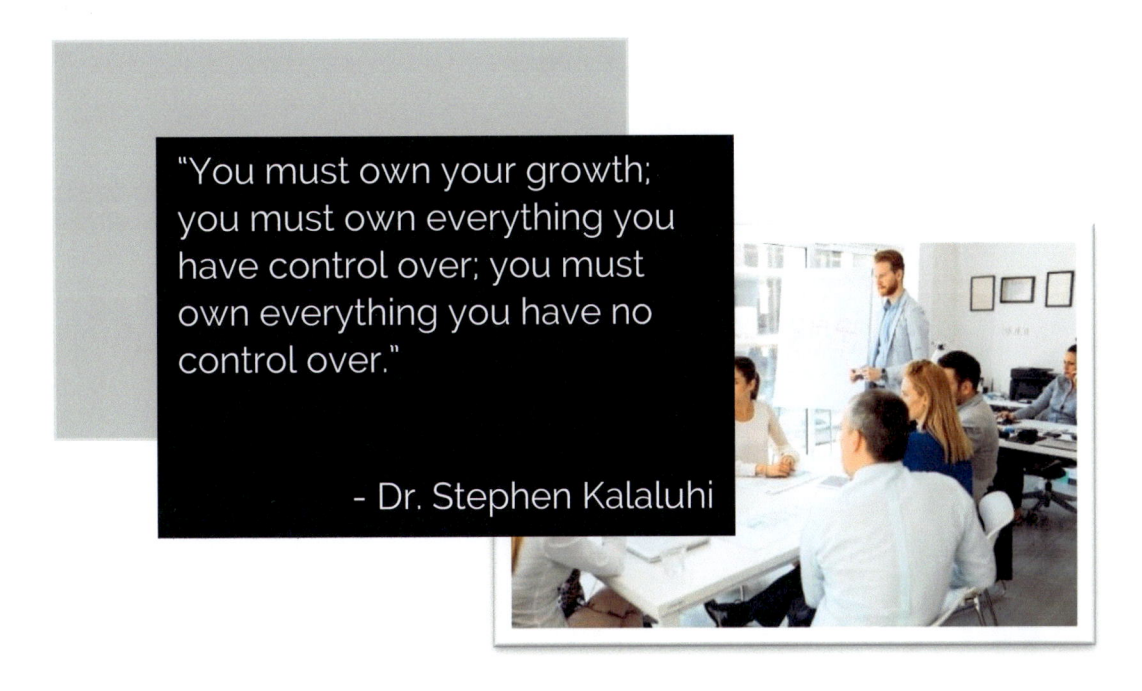

Accountability is in such disarray in today's corporations because there's no gray zone when it comes down to it – you either are accountable, or you are not. As a leader, it is important to recognize this truth in your daily actions and your daily communications. You are either accountable to your people or you are not. You are either accountable to keeping your word or you are not. You are either accountable to continuous growth or you are not. There is no in-between and there is no "almost." These absolutes make it difficult for leaders to stay accountable and many, therefore, stop trying altogether.

KEY # ①:

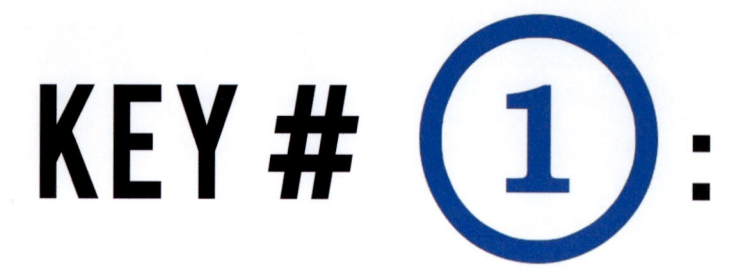

Be Clear

THE WHAT

Summarize conversations to create clarity within your team.

and...

THE WHY

Summarizing conversations creates builds accountability within organizations because it takes the conversation from casual talk to executable action items.

Who is responsible for what? By when does it need to be completed? To whom does progress need to be communicated? To whom can they turn to for support? What happens if a timeline is missed?

Your Thoughts...

EXPLAIN HOW CREATING CLARITY BUILDS ACCOUNTABILITY.

EXPLAIN HOW THIS PROCESS WILL REDUCE FRUSTRATIONS BETWEEN YOU AND YOUR TEAM.

KEY # ②:

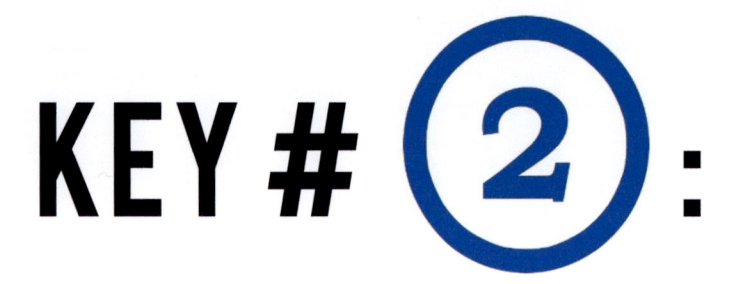

Be Real

THE WHAT

Provide truthful and honest feedback to all team members, all the time.

and...

THE WHY

Creating clarity is a great way to build accountability within your team. Ownership starts, however, when real and honest feedback is given regarding progress and growth. When your team takes ownership of their growth, or lack thereof, accountability is strengthened within your organization.

Your Thoughts...

HOW CAN YOU HOLD YOURSELF ACCOUNTABLE TO PROVIDING REAL FEEDBACK?

HOW DOES REAL AND HONEST FEEDBACK HELP YOUR TEAM GROW?

KEY # ③:

Be On-Time

THE WHAT

Out of all things that are seemingly outside of your control, the one thing you have complete control over is your time.

and...

THE WHY

Being on time, all the time, shows your commitment to the team, points to your integrity as a leader, and speaks to what you value most. Being on time all the time is a simple behavior that creates accountability within your organization because it is one of the few things that everyone has the same amount of.

Your Thoughts...

WHY IS BEING ON TIME IMPORTANT TO BUILDING ACCOUNTABILITY?

WHAT CAN YOU DO TO ENSURE THAT YOU ARE ALWAYS ON TIME?

KEY # ④:
Be Realistic

THE WHAT

Remind yourself that building accountability into the culture of your organization is a marathon. It won't happen overnight, but it will happen if you stay focused on implementing these keys.

and...

THE WHY

Building an accountability culture takes time. Keeping your word once, being on time once, owning your mistakes once, just won't do it. A culture of accountability takes time to build and it takes time to develop.

Your Thoughts...

PICK ONE THING TO FOCUS ON THIS WEEK. EVERY WEEK AFTER THIS, ADD ONE MORE ITEM TO BE ACCOUNTABLE FOR.

POSITIVE PEER PRESSURE WORKS WONDERS – CREATE A CORPORATE REWARD FOR STAYING ACCOUNTABLE.

KEY # ⑤:

Be Upfront

THE WHAT

To build a culture of accountability, you must be the first to own your mistakes. Owning your mistakes not only shows your team that you are willing to admit them, it shows your team that you are holding yourself accountable to meeting their expectations and standards.

and...

THE WHY

Stop looking at mistakes as failures, and start seeing them as opportunities for growth. Mistakes are simply processes identified that don't work. Learn from them rather than spending time trying to point fingers and assigning blame to others.

Your Thoughts...

WHY IS IT DIFFICULT FOR MOST LEADERS TO ADMIT MISTAKES?

HOW DOES ADMITTING MISTAKES INCREASE ACCOUNTABILITY?

KEY # ⑥:
Be an Owner

THE WHAT

Building a culture of accountability within your organization means you start with owning what happens within your organization. You not only take ownership of what happens within your organization, you also take responsibility for what happens within your organization.

and...

THE WHY

No matter the outcome, you must own it. The project didn't go so well? Own it. Your team failed to produce? Own it. Miss a key deliverable or due date? Own it. The more ownership you take of what happens within your organization, the more control you create around you. This is the truest essence of accountability.

Your Thoughts...

WHAT DOES OWNING OUTCOMES LOOK LIKE TO YOU?

WHY IS TAKING OWNERSHIP IMPORTANT TO BUILDING ACCOUNTABILITY?

SESSION TEN:

COURAGEOUS LEADERSHIP

10 CHARACTERISTICS OF COURAGEOUS LEADERS

> "In order for your organization to flourish and thrive, it must be led by courageous and bold leaders."
>
> - Dr. Stephen Kalaluhi

LEADERSHIP SUPPLY VS. DEMAND

Courageous leaders are few and far between in today's organizational landscape. The fear of reprisal or making a career ending mistake looms over leaders and relegates them to leading from within the status quo.

IT IS TIME FOR LEADERS TO RISE

To garner and build trust, leaders must commit to being courageous in their actions, courageous in their words, and courageous in their organizational ownership. Organizations today need leaders who are bold enough to stand for what is right, stand for what is truthful, and stand for what is needed. Leaders who exhibit courageous behaviors are quick to make the changes necessary to help their organizations thrive.

#1: COURAGEOUS LEADERS

Face Reality within Their Organizations

Courageous leaders are willing to face the realities and truths present within their organizations. Courageous leaders don't hide behind the lies and falsities because they are easier to hear. Courageous leaders get up from behind their desks and listen to what is really going on with their people.

#2: COURAGEOUS LEADERS

Seek After (and Hear) Feedback

Courageous leaders recognize they have blind spots that prevent them from growing themselves and their teams. Courageous leaders actively seek out feedback and do whatever they can to reduce or remove those blind spots as they are identified.

#3: COURAGEOUS LEADERS

Have Uncomfortable Conversations

Courageous leaders get good at having the awkward conversations that are intended to correct or align team members who are on the wrong track. Courageous leaders don't sugar-coat the truth. They don't shy away from making the necessary corrections. They don't wait for someone else to handle it for them.

#4: COURAGEOUS LEADERS

Encourage Push-Back

Courageous leaders recognize that great ideas can come from anyone, from anywhere, and at any time. Courageous leaders encourage their team members to push back on ideas if they have a better, more efficient, or more effective way of completing a task. Courageous leaders are committed to staying open to hearing about and implementing the best ideas.

#5: COURAGEOUS LEADERS

Address Under Performance

Courageous leaders don't wait for team members to become toxic before addressing performance issues. Courageous leaders are willing to do whatever it takes to protect their team from anything that might tear it apart. Under performance, behavioral issues, negative attitudes, conflict within the organization – courageous leaders take immediate action when these things arise.

#6: COURAGEOUS LEADERS

Communicate Often and Openly

Courageous leaders understand that in order for their team to make the best decisions they can, they must possess as much information as they can. This means that courageous leaders aren't scared to share information with their organization, and do so as often as possible to ensure their people are as informed as they can be.

#7: COURAGEOUS LEADERS

Are Determined to Lead Change

Courageous leaders never settle for good enough in their growth, in their organizations, in their deliverables, or in their people. Courageous leaders constantly look for opportunities to improve, and take the steps necessary to implement and execute against those improvements.

#8: COURAGEOUS LEADERS

Stand by Their Decisions

Courageous leaders stand by their decision and move forward based on their decisions. Courageous leaders understand that they must not only stand on the decisions that were made, but be brave enough to make in-course corrections, as often as is needed.

#9: COURAGEOUS LEADERS

Give More Credit to Others

Courageous leaders aren't driven by their egos. Courageous leaders are willing to give more credit to others on their teams and in their organizations than they are willing to give themselves. Courageous leaders recognize that giving credit to others is a critical component to growing an organization, and they realize that success is less about them and more about their team.

#10: COURAGEOUS LEADERS

Lead by Higher Standards

Courageous leaders don't just meet expectations and standards, they exceed the expectations and standards. They realize that to be an effective leader, they must lead from the front. This means being the first to arrive, the last to leave, and constantly setting the bar for the rest of their organization to follow.

CONCLUSION:

CONGRATULATIONS!

YOU ARE NOW A CERTIFIED INDISPENSABLE LEADER!

YOU DID IT!

Let me be among the first to congratulate you on completing your Indispensable Leader Certification Program! Your commitment to this program speaks to the value you place on leading well, and because you completed this program, everyone you influence will be positively affected.

Completing this program places you in the same ranks as some of the most elite leaders in the world. You join a community of individuals who will not stand idly by and allow the status quo to be their guide.

You are now equipped to affect positive change in every area of your life. What you choose to do with this knowledge is up to you. However, if you've come this far, I can only imagine how much further you're going to go.

Your organization needs you to be courageous; your team needs you to stand up for them when no one else can; your community needs someone they can turn to when there is no one else willing to do what everyone knows must be done. You are now that person. You are now the one your team can trust. You are now that leader your peers can turn to when they don't know what to do.

As you continue to grow and as you continue to progress, do not forget that being a great leader has less to do with you, and everything to do with serving those within your organization. They are the reason you lead, and they are the reason you completed this certification.

Here's to your continued growth and success!

Dr. Stephen Kalaluhi

CEO & Founder

The StephenK Leadership Team

Printed in France by Amazon
Brétigny-sur-Orge, FR